BEHIND THE NEWS

GLOBAL FINANCIAL CRISIS

Philip Steele

WAYLAND

First published in 2014 by Wayland
Copyright © Wayland 2014

Wayland
338 Euston Road
London NW1 3BH

Wayland Australia
Level 17/207 Kent Street
Sydney, NSW 2000

Produced for Wayland by Tall Tree Ltd
Editors: Emma Marriott and Jon Richards
Designer: Malcolm Parchment

ISBN 978 0 7502 8253 6
E-book ISBN 978 0 7502 8782 1

Dewey number: 330.9'0511-dc23

10 9 8 7 6 5 4 3 2 1

Printed in China

Wayland is a division of Hachette Children's
Books, an Hachette UK company
www.hachette.co.uk

The publisher would would like to thank the following
for their kind permission to reproduce their photographs:

Shutterstock.com unless stated otherwise:
Front cover: Getty Images, © Charles O'Rear/Corbis,
© Stefania Mizara/Corbis
© AFP/Getty Images (4), arindambanerjee (5),
Georgios Kollidas (6), WIKI_Commons (7), Olivier Le
Queinec (8), Ververidis Vasilis (9), Getty Images (10),
Frontpage (11), Getty Images (12), Kzenon (13 – posed
by models), AFP/Getty Images (14), meunierd (15), Nicku
(16), Getty Images (16), Blanscape (17), WIKI_Commons
(17), Shchipkova Elena (18), Nata789 (19), Murat
Baysan (20), Ververidis Vasilis (21), Bloomberg via
Getty Images (22), WIKI_Commons (23), WIKI_Commons
(24) del.Monaco (25), Kostas Koutsaftikis (27),
© MAL Langsdon/Reuters/Corbis (28),
© mirrorimage photos/Demotix/Demotix/Demotix/
Corbis (29), WIKI_Commons (29), Andrew Zarivny
(31), cozyta (32), WIKI_Commons (33), © CARLOS
BARRIA/Reuters/Corbis (34), Lewis Tse Pui Lung
(35), © Nevada Wier/Corbis (36), chungking (37),
lev radin (38), 1000 Words (39), Kostas Koutsaftikis
(40), © YIORGOS KARAHALIS/Reuters/Corbis (41),
joyfull (42), WIKI_Commons (43), spirit of america
(44), WIKI_Commons (45).

CONTENTS

Crunch and bust.........................4

The longer view 6

How things went wrong...........8

The home loans trap, 2008 ...10

Who was to blame?.................12

The rise and fall of prices......14

Four economic theories...........16

How secure is our money? 18

The problems with banks...... 20

Lehman Brothers, 2008........ 22

What is the best response? .. 24

Introducing austerity 26

Benefit cuts, UK, 2013 28

Should we spend or save? 30

The global impact.................. 32

Redundancies, China, 2008 .. 34

Is globalisation the answer? 36

Poverty and justice 38

Social issues, Greece, 2008- . 40

What is the answer? 42

Betting on futures................. 44

Glossary 46

Index 48

CRUNCH AND BUST

The 1990s and 2000s were times of great economic change. In the world's most developed countries, factories and mines were being run down. The really big money was now being made in finance, banking and real estate (property). Multi-national corporations were now richer and more powerful than some nations. In financial centres, such as the City of London and New York's Wall Street, fortunes were being made. The money flowed freely.

The big plunge

From 2007 onwards, the headlines told a very different story. The US housing market was now in trouble with failed payments on home loans. Banks were going bust. Businesses could not borrow the money they needed to survive. Unemployment was rising, factory production was falling, stock markets were diving. Now the media were using words like 'credit crunch',

Traders in São Paulo, Brazil, sell dollars on 15 September 2008, the day of the USA's biggest ever bank failure.

In 2012, people around the world protested against government cut-backs and the actions of the banks.

'downturn' and 'recession'. A global recession set in, the worst since the Great Depression of the 1930s. This led to a financial crisis in Europe, where the chosen remedy was a harsh cut-back in public services. People were suffering.

What next?

By 2014, there were hopes of a recovery beginning, but many jobs had been lost and the standard of living had fallen. The future was far from certain.

Had fundamental problems really been fixed, or just plastered over? Was a new home loans crisis on the way?

In this book, we go behind the headlines to find out what went wrong, what was done about it and whether that worked. Does the current global economic system make sense? Is it fair? Is it sustainable in the future, or are more crashes on the way? In a globalised economy, these questions affect everyone on the planet.

THE FALL-OUT

- By 2013, house prices in the USA were 30 per cent below their high in 2006.
- Between 2007 and 2013, about 20 per cent of Americans had lost their jobs at some point. About 25 per cent had lost as much as 75 per cent of their wealth.
- It was estimated in 2013 that by 2030 nearly 85 per cent of working-age adults in the USA will have experienced periods of economic insecurity.

THE LONGER VIEW

The financial world has evolved over thousands of years, from the days of bartering for goods to the rise of banking in the 1400s. By the 1600s, global trade and the financial institutions we know today were beginning to take shape.

Scottish economist Adam Smith advocated a system of economic self-interest.

disastrous South Sea Company bubble of 1711–20 in Britain.

• In 1776, Scottish economist Adam Smith wrote that economic self-interest spurs on wider social benefit. His theories were put to test during the Industrial Revolution and the age of empires.

• The economic system now depended on the accumulation of wealth (capital), competitive markets and waged labour. From 1846, the German economist Karl Marx declared that capitalism, based on exploitation of the workforce, was unsustainable.

• The first stock exchange was founded in Amsterdam in 1602. The Bank of Stockholm in Sweden was issuing banknotes by 1661. Economic 'bubbles' – hyped-up stock valuations, which then 'burst' – became common, notably the

• After World War I (1914–18), Germany experienced hyper-inflation. By 1923, US$1 was worth 4,210,500,000,000 German Marks. In 1929, the Wall Street

A crowd of anxious depositors gathers in the rain outside the Bank of United States after its failure in 1930.

Crash of the US stock market marked the start of the ten-year Great Depression, creating massive unemployment.

• In the 1930s, the English economist John Maynard Keynes said that capitalism could only survive depressions if governments were prepared to step in, borrow money and spend it, creating jobs in the public sector. He supported policies similar to those introduced by F D Roosevelt in the USA, under the 'New Deal'.

• In 1944–45, an international agreement made at Bretton Woods in the USA established an International Monetary Fund (IMF). International exchange rates were tied to the US dollar and its value in gold. This 'gold standard'

came to an end in 1971 when the dollar became a 'fiat' currency (no longer tied to its value in gold).

• In the 1980s, Keynesian economics were widely abandoned for the 'monetarism' of US economist Milton Friedman. Central banks could print money to tackle inflation, which was now seen as the chief problem rather than unemployment. Financial markets were subjected to less control, public services were privatised.

• In the 1990s and 2000s, electronic technology was changing the way we work, but new Internet businesses were over-valued in a 'dot-com bubble', which burst in 2000.

HOW THINGS WENT WRONG

In the 1990s and 2000s banks were eager for quick profits. Some made risky investments or cut corners. When there was a housing boom, mortgages were given to people on low incomes. Few questions were asked as to whether they could afford the monthly repayments. These were called 'sub-prime' loans.

Toxic debts

In 2004–06, US interest rates began to rise sharply. Many people could no longer afford their mortgage repayments and their houses were repossessed. These bad debts still had the potential to make money for creditors, and so they were often bundled up and sold on to other banks and investors. These so-called 'toxic debts' turned out to be a fatal liability.

Going broke

In 2007, the US sub-prime specialist New Century Financial went bankrupt.

A notice on a house in the USA shows that this property has been repossessed by the bank after the owner failed to keep up with mortgage repayments.

BANK OWNED

NO TRESPASSING

FOR INFORMATION REGARDING THIS PROPERTY OR ANY OTHER BANK-OWNED REAL ES-
TATE HOLDINGS, PLEASE CONTACT THE FINANCIAL INSTITUTION DIRECTLY AT THIS NUM-
BER: 000-000-0000.
TO VISIT THIS PROPERTY, YOU MAY CONTACT A LICENSED REAL ESTATE BROKER OF YOUR
CHOICE. THIS IS A NOTICE OF NON-JUDICIAL FORECLOSURE SALE. THIS IS NOT A TAX SALE
OR A SHERIFF SALE. NOTICE IS HEREBY GIVEN TO THE PUBLIC THAT A FINANCIAL INSTITU-
TION HAS TAKEN OWNERSHIP OF THIS PROPERTY. DO NOT REMOVE THIS NOTICE.

Greeks protest against tax hikes imposed by the central banks in September 2012.

The global investment bank Bear Sterns failed as well. Banks ran short of funds and were no longer able to borrow from other banks. In the UK, there was a 'bank run' on the Northern Rock, as panicking customers queued to withdraw their savings. In 2008, there were more financial earthquakes. In the USA, Lehman Brothers bank went bankrupt. The UK's major banks Lloyds TSB, RBS and HBOS all needed government intervention.

The house of cards

In Iceland, all three main banks collapsed, leaving their international investors in deep trouble. Ireland's economy took a five-year dive. The European Union (EU), the IMF, and the European Central Bank (ECB) bailed out the Irish economy, but wanted harsh cut-backs in spending. By 2009, world growth had shrunk to 0.5 per cent, the lowest since World War II. World unemployment hit a record high.

A national or 'sovereign' debt crisis spread across Europe, taking in those countries that used the Euro as currency. The countries of Southern Europe – Spain, Italy and especially Greece – were hit very hard. Repeated bailouts from the central banks had very harsh conditions attached. Unemployment soared and protestors took to the streets.

'In my view, the crisis wasn't an accident. We didn't get unlucky. The crisis came because there have been a lot of bad practices and a lot of bad ideas.'

David Einhorn, Greenhorn Capital.

THE HOME LOANS TRAP, 2008

Companies that sold mortgage deals to those who could not afford to pay them back made a fortune during the housing boom, but this practice eventually triggered the global financial crisis. There were probably as many US mortgage foreclosures in the years 2006–13 as during the Great Depression (see page 7).

NEWS FLASH

Date: 1 October 2008
Location: Akron, Ohio, USA
The victim: Addie Polk
The problem: Mortgage foreclosure

An advertisement for mortgage broker Fannie Mae shown at the 2008 Mortgage Banker's Association .

A sign of the times

Americans were shocked when in 2008 two government-sponsored enterprises, the Federal National Mortgage Association (known as Fannie Mae) and the Federal Home Loan Mortgage Corporation (known as Freddie Mac) had to be taken under tight government control. It was a sign that the sub-prime market had reached crisis point.

The tragedy of Addie Polk

In 2004, a woman in her late 80s called Addie Polk took out a mortgage with

The headquarters of mortgage-lender Freddie Mac in Virginia. By 2008 it was under state control.

Countrywide Home Loans on the house she had bought with her late husband Robert back in 1970. It was for US$45,620 at a rate of 6.375 per cent, over a 30-year term. Addie failed to keep up with her mortgage payments, and sheriff's deputies had posted notices of eviction on her door over 30 times. By 2008, Addie, a deaconess at her local church, was desperate. The mortgage debt was now in the hands of Fannie Mae.

Rather than face eviction, Addie tried to shoot herself in the chest while sheriff's deputies waited outside. A neighbour found her lying on her bed with a shoulder wound. She was taken to hospital. Fannie Mae set aside the debt, but Addie died from an unrelated cause the following spring. She was aged 91.

Guilty of fraud

In 2013, Countrywide was found guilty of fraud in its selling on of sub-prime debts to Fannie Mae and Freddie Mac, a deal which had hit these enterprises with a loss of US$848 million.

'It appears they're evicting her over her mortgage. She's lived in the house, the neighbours said, something like 38 years and in the last couple of years fell prey to some predatory lending company or financial institution...'

Akron police spokesman Lieutenant Rick Edwards (Reuters).

WHO WAS TO BLAME?

In the years before the financial crisis, critics of economic policy were often dismissed as prophets of gloom and doom. So why had the economists not seen it coming? If economics was a precise science, was it possible that the economists had not been very rigorous in their analysis?

Money misused?

So who was to blame? The economists, for their lack of foresight? There was a long list of suspects. At the top of the list were the banks and the finance companies. The criticisms levelled at them varied from recklessness to carelessness, from greed to outright fraud. Many of these claims were hard to dismiss, but was it fair to criticise banking as a whole?

Politics and the public?

Perhaps governments were to blame for overspending and running up sovereign debt? Had governments been so keen to encourage financial success that they failed to regulate the banks properly or tackle fraud? Was it the central banks who were the villains for misguided policies? Or were they the heroes who bailed out sovereign debt and prevented total

In 2009, the Edinburgh home of Fred Goodwin, former head of RBS, a mismanaged UK bank, was vandalised by protestors after RBS was bailed out by the taxpayer.

Banks offered easy credit to people wanting to buy pricey household goods such as cars.

meltdown? Were there systemic problems with the Euro, a new currency which had only been introduced in 1999?

Or was the public really to blame? Had they not binged on credit card purchases and taken on mortgages they could not afford? Who were they to point the finger at the bankers? It is quite possible that many or all of these factors played a part. We have to consider all possibilities in order to find out what did go wrong and to stop it happening again.

'It's not capitalism that has been the problem, but irresponsible governments and politicians who have allowed the financial system to explode by permitting the build-up of ludicrous amounts of debt...'

Chris Gibson-Smith' chairman of the London Stock Exchange

DEBATE

Should banks and other financial institutions be more tightly regulated?

YES

Irresponsible and sometimes fraudulent management was responsible for the global financial crisis.

NO

Too many rules and regulations get in the way of enterprise and the creation of wealth.

THE RISE AND FALL OF PRICES

Is the problem simply one of managing the current economic system better? Or does it need reform, perhaps even a wholesale economic revolution? The capitalist system is by its nature unstable, because that is how money is made. Speculators make their wealth by betting on the market's ups and downs.

Lastminute.com celebrates its launch in 2000. Within a day its stock value had risen 34 per cent.

DOT-COM BUBBLE

During the dot-com bubble between 1999 and 2001, companies could cause their stock prices to increase by simply adding an 'e-' prefix to their name or a '.com' to the end. A combination of circumstances created an environment in which many investors were willing to overlook traditional guides in favour of basing confidence on technological advancements.

When prices rise...

The 'free market' system is misleadingly named, for in practice it is mostly managed or manipulated by central banks or governments. It is they who try to regulate inflation – the rate at which the price of goods and services increases. If prices rise too quickly, people can no longer afford to purchase goods and services, so company profits fall. If workers are paid more, then a company's production costs rise and the prices it charges for its goods may rise. This can kick off an inflationary spiral.

When prices fall...

If prices become unrealistically high, such as during a housing 'bubble', a crash may follow. People who are paying off home loans may find that they are still paying high rates of interest while the value of the property is actually falling. The levels of unpaid debts increase.

When prices slide, this is called deflation. People will put off spending cash and buying new goods until the prices bottom out. Companies can no longer sell their products, so profits fall. They lay off workers to reduce the wages bill, so unemployment rises. The gross domestic product (GDP, the total value of goods produced and services provided within one country over a year) falls. GDP is a measure of a nation's economic growth or decline. An extended period where there is a lack of growth is one measure of a recession. Some economists define a recession as lasting for at least two financial 'quarters', that is six months, in succession. Another measure of recession is the level of unemployment.

'The Law of Inflation: Whatever goes up will go up some more.'

Anonymous.

Factory workers laid off in Seoul, South Korea, protest against redundancy in 2013. The crash following a 'bubble' in one sector, such as housing, can affect the entire economy.

FOUR ECONOMIC THEORIES

Over the centuries, economists have been sharply divided in their views about money, work, production, inflation, unemployment and social justice. The global financial crisis has focused attention on four economic thinkers in particular.

Adam Smith (1723–1790)

Known as the father of economics, Adam Smith valued commercial competition and believed that self-interest worked for the greater good of all. Smith championed free markets and believed that if they were left to themselves they would achieve a natural balance.

Smith believed free markets made societies fairer. He did not foresee the extreme inequalities that can arise in modern markets.

Karl Marx (1818–1883)

Karl Marx said that capitalism was unjust and unsustainable. He described how capitalists own and control the means of production and in that way exploit the working class who actually produce the goods. Profit should rightfully belong to the workers, who should seize the means of production for themselves. Only conflict between the classes would lead to social progress.

Keynes saw that unemployment could reduce demand so much that no jobs could be created.

John Maynard Keynes (1883–1946)

John Maynard Keynes was a capitalist who helped to plan the World Bank and the IMF. He had foreseen the dangers of hyper-inflation and the Great Depression in the 1920s and 30s (see page 7). He believed that government had a duty to take control of the economy and reduce unemployment through its fiscal policy (taxation and public spending). He did not trust the markets to regulate themselves.

Milton Friedman (1912–2006)

Milton Friedman believed that the key to success was tight control of the amount and price of money in the economy, a theory called monetarism. From the 1980s, many governments were influenced by his ideas. They deregulated banks and financial services, encouraged free trade and open markets. They transferred public services into private ownership ('privatisation').

The University of Chicago, where Milton Friedman taught, is closely associated with his theory of 'monetarism'.

Friedman believed that governments should do little except control the money supply.

HOW SECURE IS OUR MONEY?

Is the global economic system of the 21st century built on shaky foundations? Are financial crises the result of ongoing flaws in structure or policy?

'In the absence of the gold standard, there is no way to protect savings from confiscation through inflation. There is no safe store of value.'

Alan Greenspan, Chairman of the US Federal Reserve.

For much of the 20th century, the value of currency was tied to a fixed quantity of gold.

Made-up money

Some economists trace systemic problems back to the Bretton Woods agreement of 1944–45 and its ending in 1971, when the US dollar and the world's major currencies were cut adrift from any gold standard (see page 7). Money no longer had any intrinsic value, other than that assigned to it by governments and central banks. The value of savings could not be guaranteed. When governments got in a fix, they could now just print more money, making inflation more likely.

Inflation and growth

Governments need to prevent serious inflation spirals, but they also have to maintain a degree of low-level inflation in order to prevent the economy stagnating. They want growth – everyone wants growth. But perhaps the crucial question is how much growth do we all actually need? Is growth the correct measure of success? Isn't it logical to say that on a planet with limited resources, continuous growth cannot be sustained forever?

Neo-liberal failure?

In the 1980s, many nations gave up on the fiscal approaches of John Maynard Keynes, in which governments intervened to create jobs. They now followed the 'neo-liberal' policies of Milton Friedman, reducing government intervention and letting market forces rule the day. The strategy was to limit trade union powers and workers' rights, to cut the workforce, but at the same time increase productivity. Companies would become more profitable and returns on investment would improve. Banks and financial institutions were freed from regulations that held back their profits.

The great recession was the final proof that the neo-liberal experiment had failed, said some – but others still held on to it as the long-term solution.

Neo-liberalism is associated with high-risk, high-reward banking known as 'casino capitalism'.

'By a continuing process of inflation, government can confiscate, secretly and unobserved, an important part of the wealth of their citizens.'

John Maynard Keynes.

THE PROBLEMS WITH BANKS

We use the word 'bank' to describe all sorts of institutions. A central bank is a financial hub which controls interest rates and manages the money supply. Investment banks provide financial services, while retail banks deal with everyday transactions, savings, personal or business loans.

Emergency measures

As the global financial crisis tightened its grip, central banks took various measures to halt the recession. One remedy was called quantitative easing (QE). Central banks tried to stimulate the economy by increasing the quantity of money available. They did this by buying out long-term bonds or securities from banks and other financial institutions, so that these would then have enough funds to lend to other businesses – and get the economy moving. As a policy, it needed careful balancing. Too much easing could cause hyper-

The policy of quantitative easing means printing money to prevent any fall in the money supply.

inflation. Not enough, and the banks might refuse to lend. Did it work? Some economists say it had little impact, but the IMF felt that it did prove to be worthwhile.

Too much power?

As the sovereign debt crisis spread through Europe after 2009, central banks bailed out not just companies but whole countries, imposing extremely harsh conditions in return for massive transfusions of money. This averted disaster, but revealed just how much power central banks now held over national governments. As independent institutions, central banks were not accountable to the public and had no democratic mandate. Was capitalism really about economic and political freedom, as Milton Friedman had claimed, or just a dictatorship of international bankers?

Greek teachers demonstrate against the job cuts demanded by the country's international creditors in 2012. Greece was hit especially hard by austerity measures.

'We have suffered dramatic wage cuts, but we are not fighting for money or privileges. We are fighting to save education'

Thomai Pagiantza, teacher at an elementary school in Alexandria, northern Greece.

LEHMAN BROTHERS, 2008

It was said that Lehman Brothers Bank was too big to fail. After all, it was the fourth-largest investment bank in the United States. It had a long track record of success, having survived the Wall Street Crash of 1929 and the Great Depression of the 1930s.

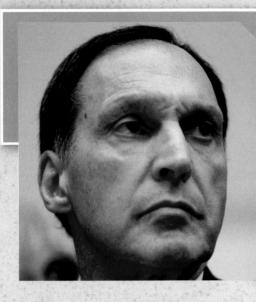

NEWS FLASH

Date: 15 September 2008
Locations: New York City and global
The firm: Lehman Brothers Holdings Inc.
The boss: Richard S Fuld Jr.
The problem: Bankruptcy

Richard S Fuld Jr, the CEO of Lehman Brothers, was known on Wall Street as 'the Gorilla' for his combative style.

Going down

In the years 2003–05, Lehman Brothers acquired five mortgage lending companies, including a sub-prime specialist. They made record profits – until the housing market fell apart. In 2008, the companies failed and Lehman shares fell by 42 per cent. The US government decided not to intervene, but the firm had over US$600 billion of debt, so it filed for bankruptcy, the largest in US history. Almost 26,000 employees faced losing their jobs. Over 4,000 of these were in the City of London, where streams of anxious men and women left their

A cluster of sub-prime mortgage failures left Lehman Brothers with debts far larger than its capital.

offices in Canary Wharf clutching boxes with their personal possessions.

The knock-on effect

The Lehman Brothers crash affected investors around the world and hit other major banks, such as the Royal Bank of Scotland (RBS) and HBOS, the UK's biggest mortgage lender. The stock market see-sawed, confidence drained away. It was confirmation that this was a crisis on an epic scale. The US government had to change its mind about bail-outs as further financial institutions floundered.

Bonus bonanza

The fall of Lehman Brothers gave banking a bad name. It was soon discovered that the company had been cooking its books – dodgy accounting had been used to conceal massive debts. Meanwhile, executives had left with huge payouts. It was also revealed that the hard-nosed Chief Executive Officer, Dick Fuld, had in the year before the bankruptcy earned a basic salary of US$750,000, plus a cash bonus of US$4,250,000 and stock worth US$16,877,365.

'Your company is now bankrupt, our economy is in crisis, but you get to keep $480 million. I have a very basic question for you, is this fair?'

US Representative for California Henry Waxman (Democrat), to Lehman CEO Richard Fuld.

WHAT IS THE BEST RESPONSE?

Commentators argued that the reckless pursuit of profit by investment bankers was at the heart of the crisis. Bankers would borrow money to buy more assets, hoping that their gains would outpace their debts, a process known as leverage. Too much leverage put company profits at risk.

> 'The Government bailed out the people and imprisoned the banksters – the opposite of what America and the rest of Europe did.'
>
> Ólafur Ragnar Grímsson, President of Iceland.

After the 2008 crisis, Icelandic president Grímsson criticised other countries' lack of help to Iceland.

How did governments respond?

Governments temporarily nationalised some troubled banks (becoming the chief shareholder). This meant that they could inject public money and restructure the banks, placing a firewall between everyday transactions and the bad debts. Iceland let its big banks go bust and refused to honour their debts, a policy which was praised by financial commentators.

Bash the bankers?

Public opinion was already infuriated by the high salaries and bonuses of the bankers.

THE BANKS OWN YOU!
THE GOVERNMENT HAS A CREDIT CARD WITH NO LIMIT
AND YOU ARE THEIR COLLATERAL!
WE ARE THE 99%
OCCUPYLONDON.ORG.UK — TWITTER.COM/OCCUPYLSX

DRAGON Represents
FREE MASONS, THEY ARE
SECRET SOCIETY WITH RULERS
MASTERS, APPRENTICES etc
TAL OVER 7 MILLION
WIDE. THEY ARE IN THE
VERFUL POSITIONS — ROYALTY

Public backlash against the banks' behaviour grew in 2011. Here, protestors stage a sit-in outside St Paul's Cathedral, London, 2011, which some of the Cathedral's clerics supported.

Many people became even angrier when taxpayers' money was used to bail out the banks. From 2014, the EU brought in caps on bankers' bonuses, a move resisted by the UK Government which feared it would drive business away from the City of London. New bodies were created to regulate all aspects of UK banking in 2013, but only time will tell if they are effective.

Financial crime

So was the crisis really down to over-enthusiastic wheeling and dealing?

Or did the rot go deeper? Some banks had been engaging in false accounting or fraud. In 2012, it was discovered that Barclays had been collaborating with other banks to rig the Libor (London Interbank Offered Rate), in order to boost their credit rating. This might have affected trillions of dollars' worth of business in the USA.

There were calls for financial crime to be dealt with more severely in the UK courts. The US system was already more prepared to send fraudsters to jail.

DEBATE
Should bankers be paid big bonuses?

YES

If you want to attract the best people, you have to pay big rewards.

NO

Bankers should be just paid for the job they do, as in every other job.

INTRODUCING AUSTERITY

The financial crisis had already caused hardship around the world. With the sovereign debt crisis in Europe, the sickness broke out in a high fever. The IMF, the European Central Bank, the EU and the British Government all prescribed austerity. For opponents, this was the sort of cure that could kill the patient.

Kill or cure?

Economic austerity means a severe cut-back in public spending by central, regional or local government. Savage austerity cuts were made across southern Europe and in Ireland during the financial crisis, and to a lesser degree in the United States. In the UK, the aim was to reduce the rate at which the government borrows money. The difference between government income and expenditure is called the budget deficit.

GREEK UNEMPLOYMENT RATE, BY AGE GROUP, OCTOBER 2007–2012 (%)

	2007	2008	2009	2010	2011	2012
15–24	22.9	22.1	28.5	34.7	46.7	56.6
25–34	11.6	10.6	13.0	18.9	27.0	34.1
35–44	6.3	6.1	8.3	11.6	15.9	23.3
45–54	4.5	4.5	6.9	9.3	14.2	19.5
55–64	3.1	3.1	4.9	6.8	9.0	15.4
65–74	1.4	0.8	1.0	1.9	3.6	4.9
Total	8.1	7.5	10	13.8	19.7	26.8

Source: Greek Statistical Authority, January 2013

Austerity measures in Greece led to violent social unrest. Here, youths hurl stones at police in Athens, 2008.

Ongoing austerity policies aimed at deficit reduction involved privatising public services, introducing or increasing charges for services and reforming the system to make it harder for people to claim welfare benefits for unemployment or disability, for example.

Where's the catch?

Critics of austerity complained that cutting public services would also hit industrial recovery. If library services were cut for example, publishers would be able to sell fewer books. If fire brigades were cut, then firms making fire-fighting equipment would become less profitable. Workers who lose their jobs at a time of high unemployment would need to claim benefit, which is another cost to the government. Some opponents made political criticisms of the kind of cuts that had been targeted. Why close hospitals, said some, when we could get rid of hugely expensive and outdated nuclear weapons programmes?

'The situation that the workers are undergoing is tragic and we are near poverty levels'

Greek trade unionist Spyros Linardopoulos, interviewed by the BBC.

BENEFIT CUTS, UK, 2013

Linda Wootton lived in Rayleigh, a town to the east of London. She was 49 years old. Because she had been declared unfit for work, she received a benefit payment of £130 per week. Linda had received two heart and lung transplants and had to take 10 different prescription drugs a day.

NEWS FLASH

Date: 24 April 2013
Locations: Rayleigh, Essex, England
The problem: Reassessment of welfare benefit
The victim: Linda Wootton

Bernard Bourigeaud, the CEO of Atos, the IT firm that won a controversial contract in UK healthcare.

Welfare cuts

The UK government decided to reassess all claimants like Linda as part of their drive for austerity. They believed that many of them were really fit for work, and that they were defrauding the government of a lot of money. Stories in the press often told of 'scroungers' who abused the system. Respondents to a survey of the public suspected that probably 27 per cent of the UK's total welfare budget was lost to fraudulent claims. The real figure? According to official statistics it was just 0.7 per cent.

Fit to work?

In 2014, Linda was called in for reassessment. The service had been privatised and was now operated by a private company called Atos, whose chief executive earned £44,000 per week. Despite testimony from her doctors, Linda was declared to be fit for work, and her benefit was stopped. Her appeal was rejected. Nine days later, on 24 April 2013 Linda Wootton died of kidney failure, lung and heart problems and high blood pressure. An uncommon case? Far from it: by January 2013 1,300 people in UK had died after they had been told to prepare to return to work, and 2,200 had died before the assessment could be completed at all.

A disabled activist demonstrates against Atos in London in 2011. Appeals against 37 per cent of Atos's work capability assessments were successful.

'It took half an hour for her to die – and that's a woman who's 'fit for work'. The last months of her life were a misery because she worried about her benefits, feeling useless, like a scrounger.'

Peter Wootton, Linda's husband.

ASSESSING PEOPLE

Atos took part in the widely derided Work Capability Assessment for the UK government's Department for Work and Pensions (DWP). The company was heavily criticised, particularly for the way it implemented the DWP's criteria for the treatment of disabled people.

SHOULD WE SPEND OR SAVE?

The big political argument of the last few years has been whether austerity actually works. Some say it is just common sense. Isn't attacking the budget deficit really a question of balancing the books? And that surely is a basic principle of good housekeeping?

'Well obviously the economy is critical to everything we do and we need to get the economy back in shape, the deficit down, the debt paid off, so that the economy can grow again and grow properly.'

Iain Duncan Smith, UK Secretary of State for Work and Pensions (Conservative).

To cut, or not to cut?

Followers of the economist John Maynard Keynes claim that the time to bring in an austerity programme is once growth is forging ahead. During a slump, the government should be spending its way out of debt. Public spending creates jobs, giving people more money to spend on goods and thereby boosting the economy, which will then expand. Only then is it the time to reduce borrowing.

Better times ahead?

So who is being proved right? Economic forecasts from late 2013 and early 2014 had some good news for the UK's Conservative Chancellor, George Osborne. Retail sales were rising more than expected. Claims for unemployment benefit were falling. Growth forecasts were up and factories were reporting stronger demand for their goods.

But was this as a result of the austerity cuts? The Bank of England had its doubts,

The Hoover Dam (1931–36) was one of the vast building projects of the New Deal, the spending plan that helped lift the USA out of the Great Depression.

'It is deeply destructive to pursue austerity in a depression.'

Nobel prize winning economist Paul Krugman.

pointing out that recovery in the UK was far behind that in the USA, where the austerity measures had been less extreme. Some economists said that it was low interest rates which were fuelling a possible recovery, and that the government had been spending more than it had planned. Might any recovery actually have been stronger without austerity cuts being imposed in the first place?

DEBATE   Does austerity work?

YES	NO
Cutting wasteful expenditure and reducing the deficit is necessary to get the economy back to good health.	*Cutting jobs reduces spending power and drives the economy back into recession.*

THE GLOBAL IMPACT

Countries around the world felt the impact of the recession. Even in the rapidly developing 'BRICS' countries (Brazil, Russia, India, China and South Africa), where growth rates had been breaking records, a slow-down had begun. As exports fell, China tried to shift its focus from exports to the home market.

Going worldwide

In Africa exports of commodities fell too, as international demand began to drop off. There were fears that international aid budgets would be cut.

The Japanese economy had already experienced its own problems of stagnation and recession ever since the early 1990s and the global recession made recovery harder. Australia seemed to weather the storm, perhaps because of its huge iron ore wealth, perhaps because of

The building boom continued unabated in China as the state encouraged consumerism.

Golden Dawn, Greece's far-right party, demonstrate outside the Greek parliament building in 2013. Riding on a wave of public resentment towards the EU, the party won three seats in the 2014 European Elections.

the fiscal policies of its Reserve Bank. However, there too by the end of 2013 there was talk of a coming recession.

Euro panic

For the Eurozone nations, the financial crisis had the impact of a tsunami. Some countries were already loaded with bad sovereign debt and were in no position to bail out their failing banks and companies without getting into even deeper trouble.

Private credit-rating companies, enjoying extraordinary power, sent major national economies into a spin just by downgrading their rating. Only the intervention of the IMF, the EU and the European Central Bank (ECB) could save the day, yet to many the austerity measures they imposed seemed intolerable.

By the middle of 2013, unemployment in both Greece and Spain had soared to 27 per cent. Resentment grew against the wealthier northern nations, such as Germany, which were demanding that their southern counterparts undergo strict austerity measures.

Political fallout

In Italy, a leading economist, Mario Monti, was appointed prime minister to head a team of unelected specialist 'technocrats' to sort out the mess. In Greece, members of a far-right party were elected to parliament. Was Europe returning to the chaos and horrors of the 1930s? Political turmoil led to abrupt changes of government across the region and damaged the stability of the EU. Would democracy survive the test?

REDUNDANCIES, CHINA, 2008

Although China was still governed by the Communist Party, it had abandoned communist economics in favour of state-sponsored capitalism. Growth had soared, but took a dip in 2008–09 because of the worldwide recession. Times became very tough for low-paid Chinese workers.

NEWS FLASH

Date: 2008

Locations: Shandong, Hubei and Guangdong provinces, People's Republic of China

The problem: Effect of the recession on Chinese exports

Outcomes: Factory closures, job losses

A man walks past a closed factory in Wenzhou, Zhejiang Province, in 2011 after the bankruptcy of the owner.

No exports, no work

The Chinese New Year or Spring Festival is a time when many Chinese working people like to go home to visit their families. City railway stations are full of migrant workers carrying bags full of gifts to take back to their villages in the countryside. However, in 2008 many were leaving the cities on a one-way ticket. Factories in the big cities were closing down. Because of the recession, overseas markets were no longer importing so many Chinese goods.

In 2008, tens of thousands of small

As growth slowed in China, workers returned to small, family owned businesses like this one in Puning, Guangdong Province.

firms closed down in the southern province of Guangdong. Even if factories stayed open, some workers had to accept a 75 per cent cut in wages. In some cases, the government stepped in with financial support for laid-off workforces.

China, on the up or down?

Growth did recover in China, which today has the world's second biggest economy after the USA. In 2013, the Chinese Government said it was prepared to have a lower growth rate, and rely more on increasing home consumption than on the export markets. Big economic and social reforms were brought in, with greater reliance on market forces than on central government planning. Was this a recipe for success or disaster? In 2014, some economists predicted success for the project, but the international financier George Soros warned that a rise in Chinese debt could open a whole new chapter in the global financial crisis.

'One day we went to work as usual, the next it was all closed... Thousands of us are looking for jobs now. We walk around every day till our feet ache but we can't find anything.'

Migrant worker Wei Sunying, a former toy factory employee in Dongguan, *The Guardian*, 2008.

IS GLOBALISATION THE ANSWER?

The IMF (see page 7) aims to promote economic cooperation between countries; the World Bank loans to developing nations, and the World Trade Organisation (WTO) regulates international trade. Perhaps the ultimate symbol of the global market is the Internet, with money trading around the world at lightning speed.

Globalisation – a blessing or a curse?

Was globalisation – the worldwide integration of markets and trade – a factor in the crisis? The downturn certainly seemed to prove the old saying that 'If America sneezes, the whole world catches a cold.' Economies around the world are now so interconnected that if one falls, they all go down like dominoes.

If there is unemployment and recession in the UK, does it make sense to outsource jobs to Bangalore in India? Supporters claim that globalisation creates wealth, encourages development and stabilises economies. Critics complain that wealth is distributed unequally, that financial interests are often placed above human rights or the environment and that minority cultures are often overwhelmed.

With improved communications technology, companies can now base their customer service centres in places where labour costs are cheaper.

Barriers to free trade?

The recession has threatened global trade in many ways. New regulations which require banks to increase their liquidity (access to funds) in order to reduce future risk, have made it harder for them to finance international trade. In the wake of recession, some politicians have come to talk of protecting national markets by introducing restrictive trade measures. This policy is called 'protectionism' and is resisted by the WTO, which insists that free trade is the best route out of recession.

Improvements in transport have been a major driver in globalisation. In Shanghai, China, the USA has invested in this 'mega-port', making it the largest in the world. It handles more than 700 million tonnes of cargo every year.

DEBATE
Should it matter that our goods are made in foreign countries?

YES

In hard times, countries should look after the interests of their own workers.

NO

The world has moved on from that position. Free trade works best when it is global.

POVERTY AND JUSTICE

The debate about the global financial crisis is often a fierce one. Many different arguments are raised. Most of these theories talk of eradicating poverty and promoting social justice – yet propose completely different economic and social remedies.

On the one hand...

Adam Smith (see page 6) wrote that self-interest acts in the interest of the common good. Many politicians today believe that equality of opportunity is a better solution than redistribution of wealth through taxation. Some people are always going to be more able than others, they say, and deserve higher financial rewards. By spending money, the rich boost the economy and create jobs. In this way, wealth 'trickles down' to the poorer levels

Volunteers distribute food at a food bank in New York in 2010 to people unable to afford the cost of feeding their families.

Protestors storm Fortnum & Mason, a luxury food store in London, to protest against tax avoidance by the rich.

of society. The chance of earning money makes others aspire to do the same. The welfare state and the culture of benefits only rewards laziness – and costs a vast amount at a time when we can ill afford it. Private firms can do the same job as public services, but more efficiently because they compete with each other.

... and on the other

Those who oppose this argument might point out that taxation can be used to make society fairer for all. At the moment, equal opportunities are only a dream. As for Adam Smith, 'self-interest' is one thing, but greed is quite another. That 'trickle down' effect is a myth. Wherever neo-liberal policies (see page 19) have been used, the result has been a sharp increase in the poverty gap. This increases the likelihood of problems such as social unrest, poor health or crime – all of which cost society dearly. An efficient welfare state is affordable and provides an essential safety net, especially important in times of recession. Cutting public services is a false economy. Privatised firms serve the interest of shareholders rather than the public. Often privatisation deals allow them to skim off profits, while leaving the public with a burden of debt.

DEBATE Should the tax system redistribute wealth to the disadvantaged?

YES

In a civilised society fiscal policy should be used to protect the poorest from hardship.

NO

The tax system should be there to reward and encourage enterprise, not to provide handouts.

SOCIAL ISSUES, GREECE, 2008–

Since 2008, Greece has received 240bn Euros in loans from the IMF, ECB and EU – but in that period the economy has shrunk by 23 per cent. Unemployment is still over 27 per cent. Whatever caused this situation, it was the Greek people who were blamed for the crisis, and they who paid the price.

NEWS FLASH

Date: 2008-2014
Location: Greece
The problem: Sovereign debt crisis
Measures imposed: Severe austerity
Outcome: Social breakdown

Tempers run high outside the Greek parliament building in 2011 as protestors vent their feelings against the EU's austerity measures.

Austerity catastrophe

Catastrophe is a word from the ancient Greek language. It originally meant an overturning, a sudden end, a fatal turning point. What have these catastrophic economic figures meant for the everyday lives of modern Greeks? Austerity of a kind normally seen only in wartime. Taxation was increased on income, property, purchases and fuel. Public sector jobs were cut and wages slashed. Health spending was cut by billions of Euros.

Closures or mergers were planned for 1,976 schools. Teachers' salaries were cut by about 40 per cent. The state pension age was raised, benefits were cut.

The social cost

Suicide rates rose by 40 per cent or so in the first five months of 2011. In 2012, the minimum wage was cut by 22 per cent. Charities have had to supply free food parcels. Families have broken up. Prisons have become run down and overcrowded as budgets were cut. And if austerity has been making things bad for the Greeks, it has been even worse for penniless migrants and refugees who have entered Greece from Africa or the Middle East, fleeing wars or even worse poverty. They were scapegoated for the troubles and often attacked on the street.

Jobless Greeks queue outside an employment office in 2011. In that year unemployment reached 18 per cent – 48 per cent up on the previous year.

The Greek government said that the country would officially come out of recession in 2014. But the international Organisation for Economic Co-operation and Development (OECD) was not so sure. Could the country stay in recession for more years to come?

> **'The crisis has made a bad situation worse...
> Alcoholism, drug abuse and psychiatric
> problems are on the rise and more and more
> children are being abandoned on the streets.'**
>
> **Costas Yannopoulos, from the charity Smile of the Child,
> *The Guardian*, 2011.**

WHAT IS THE ANSWER?

In history, politicians and business leaders have often caused great human suffering by pushing through all kinds of radical economic plans. They have made the facts fit their ideas, rather than the other way round. All such plans are doomed to failure because they are not sustainable on a human level.

Children scavenge for food at a rubbish tip in Ukraine in 2009. The country has about 50,000 children living on the streets.

The human factor

Economic theories may crunch numbers and talk of inflation , leverage, supply and demand – but the jargon often seems to ignore the human factor. Recession, unemployment and debt can have a devastating effect on ordinary people's lives. Did the bankers and financial whizzkids think through the consequences of their actions? Economics should always

be matched to human need. After all, do we want money to work for us, or enslave us?

Ethical behaviour?

Such questions have always been at the heart of philosophical and religious debate. Wealth, poverty, greed, and envy have raised moral or ethical questions throughout history. Periods of economic boom or bust rarely show human nature at its best.

Today, the term 'usury' usually means charging excessive interest rates on loans. At times it has meant charging any interest at all. Usury was condemned in ancient Hindu, Buddhist, Jewish, Christian and Islamic scriptures. Despite this, it became the central practice in the global financial system. Today, some Islamic banks have been founded which try to conform to original Muslim principles.

Predatory lending

Many Christian leaders condemn predatory lending to vulnerable people, such as the 'payday' loans which have become a notorious feature of the financial crisis. Payday loan companies offer unsecured short-term credit, sometimes attached to an annual percentage rate of over 1,000 per cent.

'Nowadays people know the price of everything and the value of nothing.'

Oscar Wilde, *The Picture of Dorian Gray*, 1890

BETTING ON FUTURES

The global financial crisis made many people feel a sense of great injustice. Why should the poor be targeted for mistakes made by millionaire bankers? At a time when the public were being asked to make great sacrifices, why were vastly rich multinational companies being allowed to pay less tax?

'As long as the problems of the poor are not radically resolved by rejecting the absolute autonomy of markets and financial speculation, and by attacking the structural causes of inequality, no solution will be found for the world's problems...'

Pope Francis, head of the Roman Catholic Church.

The debate goes on

As of 2014, it looked as if a recovery might take hold, at least in the UK. Had the crisis at last been resolved? Would the public concern now evaporate? The British Chancellor, George Osborne, was quick to point out that many more years of austerity cuts were still to come, so it seems that heated debate, both for and against, is likely to continue. New writers

Migrant workers arrive to pick crops in California, just as they did during the Great Depression of the 1930s.

Dorothea Lange's famous photograph taken during the Great Depression captures the despair on the face of a migrant worker.

are now arguing that inequality prevents a country from running efficiently. But are politicians listening? The gap between rich and poor grows ever wider.

Sorted or not sorted?

Concern has been expressed by many economists that the lessons of the global financial crisis have not been learned. Student textbooks have not been revised. Does that mean that it could all happen again? A novel called *The Way We Live Now* describes how greed and dishonesty can take hold of the financial system at great social cost. That book was written by Antony Trollope – back in 1875! Are we doomed to repeat past mistakes, or can the globalised world now look forward to a brighter future?

A changing world

That will depend on all sorts of unknown factors. Economic change will be affected by technological advances, by population growth or decline, by resources, by climate and environment, by political stability. Such factors will have to be allowed for, but no new economic plan will work if it is not accountable to the people whose lives it affects. Speculation on the price of future commodities is part of the financial world. It could be said that economists and politicians are betting on all our futures.

GLOSSARY

austerity

In economics, policies brought in to reduce public spending.

benefit

A public payment or concession intended to assist needy members of society under a social welfare scheme.

bonus

A one-off payment or reward made in addition to wages.

bubble

An economic crisis caused by over-valued stock and unsustainable prices.

budget deficit

The amount by which public expenditure exceeds public income.

capital

Accumulated wealth used to create further profit.

capitalism

An economic system based upon the accumulation of capital, private ownership, competition and wage labour.

central bank

A national institution that may manage gold reserves, currency, money supply and financial regulation.

crash

The sudden, disastrous collapse of a market, as in the Wall Street Crash of 1929.

credit crunch

A sudden reduction in the availability of credit from banks and lenders.

depression

A long period of economic decline or recession, sometimes defined as lasting for two years or more.

downturn

A decline in economic activity or profit.

fiscal policy

Government policy that deals with taxation and spending.

foreclosure *or* **repossession**

An attempt by a lender to recover the balance of a bad debt. For example, a bank may seize a home if its purchaser cannot keep up mortgage repayments.

fraud

Financial deception and corruption.

globalisation

The integration of economics worldwide, with trans-national corporations, rapid communications, and the movement of capital and labour across borders.

gold standard

A monetary system in which the currency is based on a fixed value in gold.

hyper-inflation

A dangerously high and rapidly increasing rate of inflation.

inflation

A long-term rise in the price of goods and the cost of living.

interest rate

The rate at which interest on borrowed money has to be paid to the creditor.

investment bank

A bank that helps people, companies or banks to raise capital.

leverage *also known as* **gearing**

Buying assets with borrowed money in the hope that the profits will exceed the debts.

monetarism

A policy that focuses on money supply.

mortgage

A loan used to buy property, secured against the value of that property.

neo-liberal economics

A modern economic policy based upon deregulation of financial institutions and privatisation of public services.

payday loans

Short-term loans from one payday to the next, often criticised for their extremely high rates of interest.

poverty gap

A measurement of poverty, defined against a base line of economic need.

privatisation

Turning publicly owned services over to private ownership.

protectionism

Regulating free international trade to support businesses in one country.

quantitative easing

A way of stimulating the economy during a financial crisis. A central bank buys up the assets of commercial banks so that they can lend more money.

recession

A period of decline in trade and industry, lasting two months or more.

redundancy

The laying off of workers who are no longer needed.

sovereign debt

Government bonds in a foreign currency, which are used to finance growth. Repayment may become problematic in a financial crisis.

sub-prime lending

High-risk loans made to people who may have trouble with repayment.

taxation

The imposition of charges payable to the state, due on private income, services, property or trade. Taxes are used to fund public works, services and welfare.

trade union *or* **labour union**

An organisation of workers that aims to protect working standards, employment, wages and conditions.

INDEX

A

Africa 32, 41
Akron 10, 11
Amsterdam 6
Atos 28, 29
austerity 21, 26, 27, 30, 31, 33, 40, 41, 44
Australia 32

B

Bank of England 30
Barclays 25
Bear Sterns 9
Bourigeaud, Bernard 28
Brazil 4, 32
Bretton Woods 7, 18
BRICS 32

C

California 23, 44
Canary Wharf 23
capitalism 6, 7, 13, 16, 19, 34
Chicago, University of 17
China 32, 34, 35, 37
City of London 22, 25
Communist Party 34

D

dot-com bubble 7, 14
Duncan Smith, Iain 30

E

ECB 9, 26, 33, 40
Edwards, Rick 11
Einhorn, David 9
England 28
EU 9, 25, 26, 33, 40
Euro 9, 13, 33, 40

F

Fannie Mae 10, 11
Freddie Mac 10, 11
Friedman, Milton 7, 17, 19, 21
Fuld, Richard S Jr 22, 23

G

Germany 6, 33
Gibson-Smith, Chris 13
globalisation 36, 37
gold standard 7, 18
Great Depression 5, 7, 10, 17, 22, 31, 44, 45
Greece 9, 21, 26, 27, 33, 40, 41
Greenspan, Alan, 18
Grimsson, Ólafur Ragnar 24
Guangdong 34, 35

H

HBOS 9, 23
Hoover Dam 31
Hubei 34
hyper-inflation 6, 17, 20

I

Iceland 9, 24
IMF 7, 9, 17, 21, 26, 33, 36, 40
India 32, 36
Industrial Revolution 6
inflation 6, 7, 14, 15, 16, 18, 19, 42
Italy 9, 33

J

Japan 32

K

Keynes, John Maynard 7, 17, 19, 30
Krugman, Paul 31

L

Lange, Dorothea 45
Lastminute.com 14
Lehman Brothers 9, 22, 23
Libor 25
Linardopoulos, Spyros 27
London 25, 28, 29, 39
Lloyds TSB 9

M

Marx, Karl 6, 16
monetarism 7, 17
Monti, Mario 33

N

neo-liberal 19, 39
New Century Financial 8
New Deal 7, 31
New York 22, 38, 43
Northern Rock 9

O

Ohio 10
Osborne, George 30, 44

P

Pagiantza, Thomai 21
Polk, Addie 10, 11
Pope Francis 44
privatisation 17, 39

Q

quantitative easing 20

R

RBS 9, 12, 23
recession 5, 15, 19, 20, 31, 32, 33, 34, 36, 37, 39, 41, 42
Roosevelt, F D 7
Russia 32

S

Seoul 15
Shandong 34
Shanghai 37
Smith, Adam 6, 16, 38, 39
Soros, George 35
South Africa 32
South Korea 15
South Sea Company bubble 6
Spain 9, 33
speculators 14
Stockholm 6
sub-prime loans 8, 10, 11, 22, 23

T

Trollope, Anthony 45

U

UK 9, 12, 23, 24, 25, 26, 28, 29, 30, 31, 36, 44
Ukraine 42
United States 22, 25, 26, 37
usury 43

W

Wall Street 4, 6, 22, 43
Waxman, Henry 23
Wei Sunying 35
Wenzhou 34
Wilde, Oscar 43
Wootton, Linda & Peter 28, 29
World Bank 17
WTO 36, 37

Y

Yannopoulos, Costas 41

Z

Zhejiang Province 34

BEHIND THE NEWS

978-0-7502-8252-9

978-0-7502-8255-0

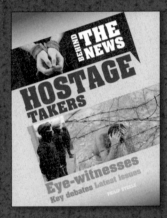

978-0-7502-8254-3

978-0-7502-8256-7

978-0-7502-8253-6

978-0-7502-8257-4

WAYLAND